# TRUMP
**Why He Lost the 2020 Election**

TRUMP: Why he lost the 2020 Election
Copyright © 2023 by REV. BARBARA M. SCHOBL-LEGEE

Published in the United States of America
ISBN    Paperback:        978-1-960629-83-8
ISBN    eBook:            978-1-960629-84-5

All rights reserved. No part of this publication may be reproduced, stored in a retrieval system or transmitted in any way by any means, electronic, mechanical, photocopy, recording or otherwise without the prior permission of the author except as provided by USA copyright law.

The opinions expressed by the author are not necessarily those of ReadersMagnet, LLC.

ReadersMagnet, LLC
10620 Treena Street, Suite 230 | San Diego, California, 92131 USA
1.619. 354. 2643 | www.readersmagnet.com

Book design copyright © 2023 by ReadersMagnet, LLC. All rights reserved.

Cover design by Ericka Obando
Interior design by Dorothy Lee

# TRUMP

## Why He Lost the 2020 Election

REV. BARBARA M. SCHOBL-LEGEE

ReadersMagnet, LLC

# ACKNOWLEDGMENT

*"I want to thank the people at ReadersMagnet for their hard work on this project. The time they spent editing, designing, and putting all the pieces together. The phone calls and emails to clarify and approve. They have done a magnificent job and deserve all the credit for the finished product.*

*Florine and Jay, I thank you from the bottom of my heart. May God Bless you and Keep You in His eternal care."*

# TABLE OF CONTENTS

PREFACE..................................................................VII

CHAPTER 1: WHERE, OH WHERE?............................1
CHAPTER 2: THE PASSAGE FROM 2 ESDRAS..........3
CHAPTER 3: AN EXPLANATION...............................12
CHAPTER 4: THE PRESIDENTS .................................20
        THE SECOND FEATHER......................24
        THE FIRST FEATHER............................26
        THE THIRD FEATHER...........................29
        THE FOURTH FEATHER......................31
        THE FIFTH FEATHER...........................31
        THE SIXTH FEATHER..........................33
        THE SEVENTH FEATHER....................35
        THE EIGHTH FEATHER......................39
        THE NINTH FEATHER .......................40
        THE TENTH FEATHER.........................41
        THE ELEVENTH FEATHER .................43
        THE TWELFTH FEATHER...................44
        THE THIRTEENTH FEATHER............48
        THE FOURTEENTH FEATHER...........50
CHAPTER 5: PRESIDENTS AFTER OBAMA..............54
CHAPTER 6: WHAT HAPPENS TO TRUMP? ............60

# PREFACE

Don't take the title as hating former President Donald J. Trump. Quite the contrary – I have never been so angry as I was when he lost the 2020 election. Angry at myself, that is.

You see, I know a lot about prophecy. I know that individual prophets can be – and have been – wrong. That is why prophets today are sometimes right – and sometimes wrong. That is why some prophets were not included in the canons of the Bible. But I know God's Word is true. Like it or not, it's true! And this prophecy has already proven itself. A lot of it has been fulfilled.

God's Word clearly says that President Trump would only serve one term, but it also states that he will never be in that office again. I should have known. And I did.

But I didn't want to accept it. I wanted, in my warped little mind, to be proven wrong. I wanted God to prove this prophecy was not about our country and, especially, not about my President. Surely Trump would win.

I looked at all the political signs. Bidens signs were less than a quarter of the signs posted for Trump. I saw the people at the Trump rallies and the people at the Biden rallies. There was no comparison! Trump should have won, hands down!

But, you ask, what am I talking about? What prophecy? Where in the Bible?

Let's take a look.

# CHAPTER 1

## WHERE, OH WHERE?

If you look in a Catholic Bible, there between the Old Testament and the New Testament, you will find the Apocrypha. That Scripture between the Testaments. The Episcopal Church also recognizes the Apocrypha as instruction, but not for doctrine. Growing up as a Baptist, I was unaware the Apocrypha existed.

In the very beginning of the Apocrypha, you will find 1 Esdras and 2 Esdras. Sometimes these are referred to as 3 Esdras and 4 Esdras. Why? At one time it was thought that Ezra wrote both the book of Ezra (also called 1 Esdras at that time) and the book of Nehemiah (also called 2 Esdras at that time). He also wrote the other two books. With that in mind, then these two books currently called 1 Esdras and 2 Esdras, would have been 3 Esdras and 4 Esdras.

Why do theologians think Ezra and Esdras are one and same?

Ezra 7:1  Now after these things, in the reign of Artaxerxes king of Persia, Ezra the son of Seraiah, the son of Azariah, the son of Hilkiah,

> *2 Esdras 1:1  The second book of the prophet Esdras, the son of Saraias, the son of Azarias, the son of Helchias, the son of Sadamias, the son of Sadoc, the son of Achitob,*

Easy answer: The same, exact, lineage. Both are the son of Seraiah, the son of Azariah, the son of Hilkiah. Yes, the spelling is slightly different, but it could the difference between Hebrew and Aramaic. It is the last letter of each name that has been changed – consistently. Seraiah to Seraias, Azariah to Azarias and Hilkiah to Helchias. Helchias is the same pronunciation as Hilkias.

OK. What does the prophecy say about Trump?

# CHAPTER 2

## THE PASSAGE FROM 2 ESDRAS

In a lot of books, writers tend to try to put America in Revelation. But there is an obscure and seldom-read selection in the Apocrypha that begins this prophecy. We begin with just the verses from 2 Esdras, in total. No interpretation nor explanation.

> *2 Esdras 10:59 And so shall the Highest shew thee visions of the high things, which the most High will do unto them that dwell upon the earth in the last days. So I slept that night and another, like as he commanded me.*

> *2 Esdras 11:1 Then saw I a dream, and, behold, there came up from the sea an eagle, which had twelve feathered wings, and three heads.*

*2 Esdras 11:2  And I saw, and, behold, she spread her wings over all the earth, and all the winds of the air blew on her, and were gathered together.*

*2 Esdras 11:3  And I beheld, and out of her feathers there grew other contrary feathers; and they became little feathers and small.*

*2 Esdras 11:4  But her heads were at rest: the head in the midst was greater than the other, yet rested it with the residue.*

*2 Esdras 11:5  Moreover I beheld, and, lo, the eagle flew with her feathers, and reigned upon earth, and over them that dwelt therein.*

*2 Esdras 11:6  And I saw that all things under heaven were subject unto her, and no man spake against her, no, not one creature upon earth.*

*2 Esdras 11:7  And I beheld, and, lo, the eagle rose upon her talons, and spake to her feathers, saying,*

*2 Esdras 11:8  Watch not all at once: sleep every one in his own place, and watch by course:*

*2 Esdras 11:9  But let the heads be preserved for the last.*

*2 Esdras 11:10 And I beheld, and, lo, the voice went not out of her heads, but from the midst of her body.*

*2 Esdras 11:11 And I numbered her contrary feathers, and, behold, there were eight of them.*

*2 Esdras 11:12 And I looked, and, behold, on the right side there arose one feather, and reigned over all the earth;*

*2 Esdras 11:13 And so it was, that when it reigned, the end of it came, and the place thereof appeared no more: so the next following stood up. and reigned, and had a great time;*

*2 Esdras 11:14 And it happened, that when it reigned, the end of it came also, like as the first, so that it appeared no more.*

*2 Esdras 11:15 Then came there a voice unto it, and said,*

*2 Esdras 11:16 Hear thou that hast borne rule over the earth so long: this I say unto thee, before thou beginnest to appear no more,*

*2 Esdras 11:17 There shall none after thee attain unto thy time, neither unto the half thereof.*

*2 Esdras 11:18  Then arose the third, and reigned as the other before, and appeared no more also.*

*2 Esdras 11:19  So went it with all the residue one after another, as that every one reigned, and then appeared no more.*

*2 Esdras 11:20  Then I beheld, and, lo, in process of time the feathers that followed stood up upon the right side, that they might rule also; and some of them ruled, but within a while they appeared no more:*

*2 Esdras 11:21  For some of them were set up, but ruled not.*

*2 Esdras 11:22  After this I looked, and, behold, the twelve feathers appeared no more, nor the two little feathers:*

*2 Esdras 11:23  And there was no more upon the eagle's body, but three heads that rested, and six little wings.*

*2 Esdras 11:24  Then saw I also that two little feathers divided themselves from the six, and remained under the head that was upon the right side: for the four continued in their place.*

*2 Esdras 11:25  And I beheld, and, lo, the feathers that were under the wing thought to set up themselves and to have the rule.*

*2 Esdras 11:26  And I beheld, and, lo, there was one set up, but shortly it appeared no more.*

*2 Esdras 11:27  And the second was sooner away than the first.*

*2 Esdras 11:28  And I beheld, and, lo, the two that remained thought also in themselves to reign:*

*2 Esdras 11:29  And when they so thought, behold, there awaked one of the heads that were at rest, namely, it that was in the midst; for that was greater than the two other heads.*

*2 Esdras 11:30  And then I saw that the two other heads were joined with it.*

*2 Esdras 11:31  And, behold, the head was turned with them that were with it, and did eat up the two feathers under the wing that would have reigned.*

*2 Esdras 11:32  But this head put the whole earth in fear, and bare rule in it over all those that dwelt upon the earth with much oppression;*

*and it had the governance of the world more than all the wings that had been.*

Now you're wondering, "What's with all the heads and the wings and the feathers?"

Let's see if we can sort this out.

We'll start out with the actual interpretation from Chapter 12.

> *Es 12:6 Therefore will I now beseech the Highest, that he will comfort me unto the end.*
>
> *2Es 12:7 And I said, Lord that bearest rule, if I have found grace before thy sight, and if I am justified with thee before many others, and if my prayer indeed be come up before thy face;*
>
> *2Es 12:8 Comfort me then, and shew me thy servant the interpretation and plain difference of this fearful vision, that thou mayest perfectly comfort my soul.*
>
> *2Es 12:9 For thou hast judged me worthy to shew me the last times.*
>
> *2Es 12:10 And he said unto me, This is the interpretation of the vision:*

*2Es 12:11 The eagle, whom thou sawest come up from the sea, is the kingdom which was seen in the vision of thy brother Daniel.*

*2Es 12:12 But it was not expounded unto him, therefore now I declare it unto thee.*

*2Es 12:13 Behold, the days will come, that there shall rise up a kingdom upon earth, and it shall be feared above all the kingdoms that were before it.*

*2Es 12:14 In the same shall twelve kings reign, one after another:*

*2Es 12:15 Whereof the second shall begin to reign, and shall have more time than any of the twelve.*

*2Es 12:16 And this do the twelve wings signify, which thou sawest.*

*2Es 12:17 As for the voice which thou heardest speak, and that thou sawest not to go out from the heads but from the midst of the body thereof, this is the interpretation:*

*2Es 12:18 That after the time of that kingdom there shall arise great strivings, and it shall stand in peril of failing: nevertheless it shall not then fall, but shall be restored again to his beginning.*

*2Es 12:19 And whereas thou sawest the eight small under feathers sticking to her wings, this is the interpretation:*

*2Es 12:20 That in him there shall arise eight kings, whose times shall be but small, and their years swift.*

*2Es 12:21 And two of them shall perish, the middle time approaching: four shall be kept until their end begin to approach: but two shall be kept unto the end.*

*2Es 12:22 And whereas thou sawest three heads resting, this is the interpretation:*

*2Es 12:23 In his last days shall the most High raise up three kingdoms, and renew many things therein, and they shall have the dominion of the earth,*

*2Es 12:24 And of those that dwell therein, with much oppression, above all those that were before them: therefore are they called the heads of the eagle.*

*2Es 12:25 For these are they that shall accomplish his wickedness, and that shall finish his last end.*

So, what does all this mean? And you've also noticed that Trump wasn't mentioned anywhere. Oh, but he was – he is just hidden in the prophecy – right along with all the other Presidents.

# CHAPTER 3

## AN EXPLANATION

The verses to be explained are given first, then, if there is an interpretation in Chapter 12, that is given, then an explanation to clarify any issues. If there is no interpretation in Chapter 12, then the verses are followed by just an explanation.

### *2 ESDRAS 10:59-11:1*

*2Es 10:59 And so shall the Highest shew thee visions of the high things, which the most High will do unto them that dwell upon the earth in the last days. So I slept that night and another, like as he commanded me.*

*2Es 11:1 Then saw I a dream, and, behold, there came up from the sea an eagle, which had twelve feathered wings, and three heads.*

## *INTERPRETATION*

*Es 12:11 The eagle, whom thou sawest come up from the sea, is the kingdom which was seen in the vision of thy brother Daniel.*

*2Es 12:12 But it was not expounded unto him, therefore now I declare it unto thee.*

*2Es 12:13 Behold, the days will come, that there shall rise up a kingdom upon earth, and it shall be feared above all the kingdoms that were before it.*

*2Es 12:14 In the same shall twelve kings reign, one after another:*

## EXPLANATION

Although it mentions 12 kings here, 2 Esdras will go on to cover more than the 12. There are also 2 little feathers:

*2Es 11:22 After this I looked, and, behold, the twelve feathers appeared no more, nor the two little feathers*

### *2 ESDRAS 11:2*

*And I saw, and, behold, she spread her wings over all the earth, and all the winds of the air blew on her, and were gathered together.*

# EXPLANATION

In the Book of Revelation, when the winds blew on the earth, it was usually a "scattering" wind. Here, we see the winds blow to gather people to this new kingdom. People want to come to this new kingdom which is represented by an eagle. With three heads. The easy answer is that our country's symbol is the eagle and our government has three heads: Executive, Judicial, and Legislative. Separate powers were set out for each branch. However, as time went by, each branch took a little of the power from one or both of the other branches. Even George Washington wrote eight Executive Orders.[1] William Henry Harrison was the only one who did not write any Executive Orders. But he was only in office for 31 days before he died of pneumonia.

That she had 12 wings related to the number of colonies. That's right – 12 and not 13.

The thirteen colonies that formed the United States of America were:

*Virginia – First Settlement in 1607*[2]

*New York – First Settlement in 1614*[3]

---

[1] https://www.presidency.ucsb.edu/statistics/data/executive-orders (Accessed 9/21/22)

[2] https://www.factmonster.com/us/us-history/states-order-entry-union#:~:text=The%20table%20below%20details%20when%20each%20state%20joined,9%2C%201788%201634%206.%20Massachusetts%20Feb.%206%2C%201788 (Accessed 9/21/22)

[3] Ibid.

*Massachusetts – 1620 at Plymouth Rock; Massachusetts Bay Colony 1630[4]*

*New Jersey – First Settlement in 1660[5]*

*New Hampshire – First Settlement in 1623[6]*

*Maryland – First Settlement in 1634[7]*

*Connecticut – First Settlement in 1636[8]*

*Rhode Island – First Settlement in 1636[9]*

*Pennsylvania – First Settlement in 1682 [10]*

*Delaware – First Settlement in 1638[11]*

*North Carolina\* – First Settlement in 1660[12]*

---

4 https://en.wikipedia.org/wiki/History_of_Massachusetts **(Accessed 9/21/22)**

5 https://www.factmonster.com/us/us-history/states-order-entry-union#:~:text=The%20table%20below%20details%20when%20each%20state%20joined,9%2C%201788%201634%206.%20Massachusetts%20Feb.%206%2C%201788 **(Accessed 9/21/22)**

6 https://connecticuthistory.org/timeline-settlement-of-the-colony-of-connecticut/ **(Accessed 9/21/22)**

7 https://www.history.com/topics/colonial-america/thirteen-colonies **(Accessed 9/21/22)**

8  https://thehistoryjunkie.com/13-colonies-list/ **(Accessed 9/21/22)**

9 https://www.americanhistorycentral.com/entries/rhode-island-colony-early-history-and-settlement/ **(Accessed 9/21/22)**

10 Factmonster.com/us/us-history/states-order-entry-union **(Accessed 9/21/22)**

11 https://www.ushistory.org/pennsylvania/pennsylvania.html **(Accessed 9/21/22)**

12 https://www.ushistory.org/pennsylvania/pennsylvania.html%20joined,9%2C%201788%201634%206.%20Massachusetts%20Feb.%206%2C%201788 **(Accessed 9/21/22)**

\* **North and South Carolina split in 1729 -** https://www.history.com/topics/colonial-america/thirteen-colonies **(Accessed 9/21/22**

*South Carolina\* –1670*[13]

*Georgia – First Settlement in 1733*[14]

It took 63 years for twelve colonies to form. It would take another 63 years for the 13th colony (Georgia) to form. That is why God said this Eagle has only twelve wings.

Vermont became the 14th State in 1791 after having been separated from New York for fourteen years and not declaring themselves a colony. Settled in 1724.

### *2 ESDRAS 11:3-4 & V. 11*

> *2Es 11:3 And I beheld, and out of her feathers there grew other contrary feathers; and they became little feathers and small.*
>
> *2Es 11:4 But her heads were at rest: the head in the midst was greater than the other, yet rested it with the residue.*
>
> *2Es 11:11 And I numbered her contrary feathers, and, behold, there were eight of them.*

---

13 Ibid.
14 Ibid.

## *INTERPRETATION*

*2Es 12:13 Behold, the days will come, that there shall rise up a kingdom upon earth, and it shall be feared above all the kingdoms that were before it.*

*2Es 12:14 In the same shall twelve kings reign, one after another:*

## *EXPLANATION*

That the head in the middle was greater than the others stands for the President of the United States. He is the most visible and people from around the world recognize who our leader is, while they probably do not know who all the members of Congress are, and probably do not know the Justices that sit on the Supreme Court.

## *2 ESDRAS 11:22*

After this I looked, and, behold, the twelve feathers appeared no more, nor the two little feathers:

## *EXPLANATION*

There are now a total of 14 feathers on the one wing. Two of them are little feathers. These are 2 Presidents who will reign but a short time.

Who are these "rulers?"

We left off with 2 Esdras 11:4, so we pick up from there.

### *2 ESDRAS 11:5-8*

*2 Esdras 11:5 Moreover I beheld, and, lo, the eagle flew with her feathers, and reigned upon earth, and over them that dwelt therein.*

*2 Esdras 11:6 And I saw that all things under heaven were subject unto her, and no man spake against her, no, not one creature upon earth.*

*2 Esdras 11:7 And I beheld, and, lo, the eagle rose upon her talons, and spake to her feathers, saying,*

### *EXPLANATION*

That she "rose upon her talons" stands for the fact this country rebelled against England. We went to war. Then we formed a separate government. One President to rule at a time.

As soon as the Convention agreed on its rules, Edmund Randolph of the Virginia delegation presented a set of fifteen resolutions, known as the Virginia Plan, which set aside the Articles of Confederation and created in its stead a supreme national government with separate legislative, executive, and judicial branches. This was largely the work of James Madison, who came to the Convention extensively prepared and well-versed in the ancient and modern history of republican government. Under the Virginia Plan, the number of representatives in each house would be determined by the population of each state. Roger Sherman proffered what is often called "the Great Compromise" (or the Connecticut Compromise, after Sherman's home state). ("The Formation of the Constitution | The Heritage Foundation") The House of Representatives would be apportioned based on population and each state would have an equal vote in the Senate. George Washington thought that it was "little short of a miracle" that the delegates had agreed on a new Constitution. Thomas Jefferson, who was also concerned about the lack of a bill of rights, nevertheless wrote that the Constitution "is unquestionably the wisest ever yet presented to men."[15]

---

[15] https://buildingblocksforliberty.org/formation-of-the-constitution/#:~:text=As%20soon%20as%20the%20Convention%20agreed%20on%20its,government%20with%20separate%20legislative%2C%20executive%2C%20and%20judicial%20branches. **Accessed 9/24/22**

# CHAPTER 4

## THE PRESIDENTS

### *2 ESDRAS 11:8*

*Watch not all at once: sleep every one in his own place, and watch by course:*

On January 7, 1789, each state was to have their electors chosen for the election of the President. That election was done on February 4, 1789. George Washington was sworn into office on April 30, 1789.[16] Each President was to "watch by course."

### *2 ESDRAS 11:9*

*But let the heads be preserved for the last.*

---

16 Ibid. Accessed 9/24/22

## *EXPLANATION*

The First United States Congress, making up the United States Senate and the United States House of Representatives, met from March 4, 1789, to March 4, 1791.[17]

And the Supreme Court was established September 17, 1789. The "heads" were "preserved for the last. Executive, Legislative and Judicial.

## *2 ESDRAS 11:10*

And I beheld, and, lo, the voice went not out of her heads, but from the midst of her body.

## *EXPLANATION*

The voice coming from "the midst of her body" would be the people. We are a representative form of government. The people speak by voting on Representatives and on various laws. Changes can be made to our Constitution only by votes of "We The People." The Legislature cannot do it. The Supreme Court cannot do. The Executive Branch (President) is not to Legislate from the Oval Office, either. Although past (and present) Presidents have done so. The Supreme Court is not to make laws by their judgments. They can only interpret the law. Either the law is Constitutionally sound, or it is not. The Legislative Branch is to make the laws. The Legislature can draft changes to the Constitution so "We

---

17 https://en.wikipedia.org/wiki/1st_United_States_Congress **Accessed 9/24/22**

The People" can vote on those changes. Then, the States have to approve or reject the changes according to the way the people in that state vote. The change to the Constitution must be proposed by a two-thirds vote of both Houses of Congress or by two-thirds of the States. A convention is then called for that purpose. The amendment must be ratified by three-fourths of the State legislatures, or three-fourths of conventions called in each State for ratification.[18]

### *2 ESDRAS 11:11*

And I numbered her contrary feathers, and, behold, there were eight of them.

### *EXPLANATION*

These "contrary feathers" will be the second group of Presidents at which we look. But we are going to look at the first group of "rulers."

### *2 ESDRAS 11:12-22*

*2 Esdras 11:12 And I looked, and, behold, on the right side there arose one feather, and reigned over all the earth;*

*2 Esdras 11:13 And so it was, that when it reigned, the end of it came, and the place thereof*

---

[18] https://www.archives.gov/federal-register/constitution (Accessed 9/24/22)

*appeared no more: so the next following stood up. and reigned, and had a great time;*

*2 Esdras 11:14 And it happened, that when it reigned, the end of it came also, like as the first, so that it appeared no more.*

*2 Esdras 11:15 Then came there a voice unto it, and said,*

*2 Esdras 11:16 Hear thou that hast borne rule over the earth so long: this I say unto thee, before thou beginnest to appear no more,*

*2 Esdras 11:17 There shall none after thee attain unto thy time, neither unto the half thereof.*

*2 Esdras 11:18 Then arose the third, and reigned as the other before, and appeared no more also.*

*2 Esdras 11:19 So went it with all the residue one after another, as that every one reigned, and then appeared no more.*

*2 Esdras 11:20 Then I beheld, and, lo, in process of time the feathers that followed stood up upon the right side, that they might rule also;*

*and some of them ruled, but within a while they appeared no more:*

*2 Esdras 11:21 For some of them were set up, but ruled not.*

*2Es 11:22 After this I looked, and, behold, the twelve feathers appeared no more, nor the two little feathers:*

### *EXPLANATION*

Some were just "puppets" for the "power behind the throne." Much as we dislike the discussion that has gone on from time to time, God's Word is true!

Now God does not always start at our beginning. So, when DID the "feathers" start? The feathers stand for the ones who "reign" – the Presidents. The clue lay in the second "feather."

# THE SECOND FEATHER

OK, this one who reigns has "a great time." This President ruled longer than any before him. And God ensured that no President would rule for that long again.

Franklin Delano Roosevelt was in office from March 4, 1933, until he died, April 12, 1945. Twelve years, one month, and eight days. He was in the beginning of his fourth term in office. Presidents since then can only be in office for a total of eight years. The twenty-second Amendment to the Constitution was ratified February 27, 1951, and limited the President to two terms in office. Further, if a Vice President served more than two years of a term to which some other person was elected President, then they may only be elected President once.

> *2 Samuel 7:28 And now, O Lord GOD, thou art that God, and thy words be true, and thou hast promised this goodness unto thy servant:*

Yes, God's Word is true.

As to what happened to this country while Roosevelt was President, he implemented the New Deal, which tried to insure the economic, social, and political benefits of American capitalism were distributed more equally among America's population.[19] Unfortunately, it did not cure the problems of the Depression. Only entry into World War II ended those problems.

The New Deal did not guarantee the right to vote and the right to a fair trial to Black people.[20]

---

19 https://millercenter.org/president/fdroosevelt/impact-and-legacy (Accessed 9/24/22)
20 Ibid.

It was under Roosevelt that the Chief Executive also became Chief Legislator, drafting policy for the U.S. That is when the White House staff grew to encompass full-time staff for domestic and foreign policy "with expertise in these areas, and a passion for governance. With enactment of the Executive Reorganization bill in 1939, FDR changed the shape of the White House forever."[21]

## THE FIRST FEATHER

With Franklin D. Roosevelt being the second, and reigned the longest, that leaves Herbert Hoover, the President preceding Roosevelt, as the first to reign in this prophecy. Why would God start with Herbert Hoover?

He was sworn in as President in 1929 – and the Stock Market Crash happened on October 28 of that year. And it affected the entire world. But there was more to it than that. Herbert Hoover was the President that came up with the plan for the "New Deal." It was then put into action by Franklin D. Roosevelt. But the Great Depression still lasted ten years.

The New Deal was supposed to give economic relief and make reforms in various areas including labor and housing, finance, agriculture, and waterpower.[22] The political

---
21 Ibid.
22 https://www.britannica.com/event/New-Deal (Accessed 9/24/22)

operative previously had been laissez-faire, which means "allow to do"[23] Folklore says it means, "leave us alone."[24]

But now government was inserting itself into many areas of the private sector. Under the agricultural New Deal, the government paid cash subsidies to farmers. This soon became payment to farms NOT to grow crops.

*The Scriptures say, "And thou shalt teach them ordinances and laws, and shalt shew them the way wherein they must walk, and the work that they must do."*[25]

The Lord did not want man to be idle.

*And withal they learn to be idle, wandering about from house to house; and not only idle, but tattlers also and busybodies, speaking things which they ought not.*[26]

He also started the Welfare Program and Food Stamps. What do the Scriptures say about this?

> *Isaiah 65:22 They shall not build and another inhabit; they shall not plant, and another eat: for as thedays of a tree are the days of my people, and mine elect shall long enjoy the work of their hands.*

---

23 https://www.britannica.com/topic/laissez-faire (**Accessed 9/24**)
24 Ibid.
25 Exodus 18:20
26 1 Timothy 5:13

*2 Thessalonians 3:10 For even when we were with you, this we commanded you, that if any would not work, neither should he eat.*

*2 Thessalonians 3:11 For we hear that there are some which walk among you disorderly, working not at all, but are busybodies.*

*2 Thessalonians 3:12 Now them that are such we command and exhort by our Lord Jesus Christ, that with quietness they work, and eat their own bread.*

That verse 11 goes right along with Exodus 18:20. They don't work and they become not only idle, but are busybodies and tattlers. God does not want His people being paid not to work. This is contrary to God's laws.

What else happened during Hoover's Presidency?

"New York City police raid the Birth Control Clinical Research Center established by Margaret Sanger, arresting two doctors and three nurses, and confiscating numerous records. Physicians and private citizens are outraged by the incident and a month later the case will be thrown out of court as a violation of a physician's right to practice medicine."[27]

---

[27] https://millercenter.org/president/herbert-hoover/key-events (Accessed 9/24/22)

What is not known by the general public is that Margaret Sanger was a racist. She started abortions because she wanted to reduce the Black and brown populations to a point where they could not "come back" to their current level of the population and overtake the whites for the majority. She placed the abortion clinics in or near the areas of greatest population of those races.

# THE THIRD FEATHER

After Franklin D. Roosevelt, arose Harry S. Truman, who started out as Roosevelt's Vice President. When Roosevelt died, Truman became President and reigned almost four years without a Vice President. He served a total of eight years.

The Constitution allows that when something happens to the President, then the Vice President takes over.[28] But the Constitution, Amendment XXV, says that if something happens to the Vice President, then the President may appoint another Vice President with confirmation by a majority vote of both Houses of Congress.[29] But the Twenty-Fifth Amendment also says that the Vice President, when ascending to the office of the President, becomes the President, and not just the Acting Vice President, as in the case of President Truman. Because Truman was only the

---
28 Constitution of the United States of America, Article II, Section 1. And Article XXV, Section 1.
29 Ibid., Article XXV, Section 2

Acting President, he could not nominate a Vice President. He was the Vice President, acting in the position of the President.

But what happens if BOTH the President and Vice President are unable to serve? The U,S, Constitution and the Presidential Succession Act of 1947 outline the presidential order of succession. The line of succession of cabinet officers is in the order of their agencies' creation.

If the President of the United States is incapacitated, dies, resigns, is for any reason unable to hold his/her office, or is removed from office, he/she will be replaced in the following order:

1. Vice President

2. Speaker of the House

3. President Pro Tempore of the Senate.

4. Secretary of State (etc. - through the 18 person, the Secretary of Homeland Security)

Truman was the President who authorized using the atomic bomb on Hiroshima and Nagasaki.

Therefore, Ezra was told, *"Behold, the days will come, that there shall rise up a kingdom upon earth, and it shall be feared above all the kingdoms that were before it."*[30]

The United States still stands as the only country to have used a radioactive bomb against another country. We were more feared than respected. I say "were" because, as I write this, Joe Biden is our President and he is not feared by any other country.

## THE FOURTH FEATHER

After Truman came Dwight David Eisenhower. He served eight years. Eisenhower was Supreme Commander of Allied forces in Western Europe during World War II. He is the only President to have criticized the atomic bombing of Hiroshima and Nagasaki. He managed Cold War-era tensions with the Soviet Union, ended the war in Korea, strengthened Social Security, and created the new Interstate Highway System. His one big failure was that he did not enforce the mandate for desegregation of schools in Brown v. Board of Education (1954).[31]

We are ALL made in the image of God.[32] Fair is fair. Wrong is wrong. Right is right. Love overcomes all.

---

30 2 Esdras 12:13
31 https://www.history.com/topics/us-presidents/dwight-d-eisenhower (Accessed 9/24/22)
32 Genesis 1: 26-27

## THE FIFTH FEATHER

John Fitzgerald Kennedy came next. He was a "little" feather because he died in office, killed by an assassin. He served for two years, ten months, and two days. Since he served less than eight years, he was the first "little feather."

He "confronted Cold War tensions in Cuba, Vietnam, and elsewhere."[33]

He met with Nikita Khrushchev to discuss the Berlin Wall. Two months later the wall started going up to divide Germany. His greatest accomplishment was the Cuban Blockade after learning the Soviet Union was building a number of nuclear and long-range missile sites in Cuba that posed a threat to the United States. The Blockade lasted two weeks and Khrushchev agreed to dismantle the sites. In exchange, we removed our missile sites from those areas close to Soviet borders. The first nuclear test ban treaty was signed with Great Britain's Prime Minister Harold Macmillan.[34]

His biggest failure was the Bay of Pigs in Cuba. On April 12, 1961, he pledged, "there will not be, under any conditions, an intervention in Cuba by the United States Armed Forces."[35] On April 17, 1961, the "intervention" started with anti-Castro Cuban exiles trained by the CIA.

---

[33] https://www.history.com/topics/us-presidents/john-f-kennedy (Accessed 9/24/22)
[34] https://www.presidency.ucsb.edu/documents/john-f-kennedy-event-timeline (Accessed 9/24/22)
[35] Ibid.

To reduce the explicit linkage with US military assistance, Kennedy chose not to authorize US air strikes. The invasion fails spectacularly."[36]

However, he escalated our involvement in Vietnam, even though he was dismayed at the situation.

September 26, 1961, he signed H.R. 9118 which created the Arms Control and Disarmament Agency. It was supposed to help create a world free of war. Then, on October 17, 1961, he called upon the Soviet Union to reconsider their decision to test a 50-megaton nuclear bomb. On October 30, 1961, they dropped that bomb at Mityushika Bay which is located north of the Arctic Circle. But Kennedy had tried.

President Kennedy also enforced the desegregation of the University of Mississippi. He said, "Americans are free to disagree with the law, but not to disobey it."[37]

# THE SIXTH FEATHER

After Kennedy came Lyndon Baines Johnson. He served the last part of John F. Kennedy's term and a four-year term of his own. His "New Deal" was the "Great Society" for all Americans. Medicare, Head Start, Voting Rights Act, Civil Rights Act.

---

36 Ibid.
37 https://communityliteracy.org/how-did-president-kennedy-respond-to-the-desegregation-of-the-university-of-mississippi/ (Accessed 9/24/22)

Medicare was started in 1965 for people over the age of 65, as well as those with Disabilities and those with end-stage kidney disease. It is funded by the Federal Government. Now I'm sure that God is not against insurance, but He is against people getting paid and not contributing anything. If I have health coverage that I pay for, and prescription drug coverage that I pay for, He does not have a problem with that. But having the government pay for everything for you makes you dependent upon the government and that is not a good thing in God's economy. I, unfortunately, am dependent upon the government for my health care needs and insurance.

> *Isaiah 55:9 For as the heavens are higher than the earth, so are my ways higher than your ways, and my thoughts than your thoughts.*

## THE SEVENTH FEATHER

After Johnson came Richard Nixon. Richard Nixon is considered the second "little" feather because he resigned and did not finish his second term in office.

Richard Nixon ushered in a time of improved relations with China.[38] Not good! We thought it was good at the time. It meant some things would be cheaper and we could afford to buy more. We could satisfy our selfishness. He who dies with the most toys ---- is still ---------- dead. Not a winner.

---
38 https://www.history.com/news/nixon-china-visit-cold-war (Accessed 9/24/22)

We can see this now. God could see it then. And He can see what comes after "now." Of course, we remember Richard Nixon for Watergate.

Nixon proposed a Family Assistance Program to provide working and non-working families with a guaranteed annual income. It was defeated in the Senate but, it helped create bit-by-bit legislations that used similar ideas – like COLAs for Social Security recipients, Supplemental Security Income (SSI), and expansion of welfare programs. He even created a revenue-sharing program with the states – "New Federalism" – that supplied billions of dollars to the states and local governments.[39] He also devalued the dollar by eight percent, placed a new tax on imports, and controls on wages and prices. All these things contributed to inflation at 8.8%.[40]

During Nixon's time in office, Roe v. Wade was decided by the Supreme Court of the United States. Although President Nixon did not decide this case, God still looks at the "ruler" of the land for things that happen. If you don't believe abortion is in the Bible, please read the following:

> *Amos 1:13 Thus saith the LORD; For three transgressions of the children of Ammon, and for four, I will not turn away the punishment thereof; because they have ripped up the women with child of Gilead, that they might enlarge their border:*

---

39 https://www.britannica.com/biography/Richard-Nixon/Election-of-1960 (Accessed 9/24/22)
40 Ibid.

This is one of a series of curses upon people who have gone against God's wishes.

Why would God feel this way?

> *Psalm 22:10 I was cast upon thee from the womb: thou art my God from my mother's belly.*
>
> *Jeremiah 1:5 Before I formed thee in the belly I knew thee; and before thou camest forth out of the womb I sanctified thee, and I ordained thee a prophet unto the nations.*
>
> *Isaiah 44:2 Thus saith the LORD that made thee, and formed thee from the womb, which will help thee; Fear not, O Jacob, my servant; and thou, Jesurun, whom I have chosen.*

"As the decision made all too clear, rights talk had displaced what had been seen as the higher concern of right versus wrong. Also missing from our contemporary cultural memory is the fact that many Republicans, as well as Democrats, welcomed Roe v. Wade as the next step in a necessary process of liberating human beings from prior constraints. Yet, we now know that even more was at stake."[41] While Herbert Hoover's administration saw the courts throw out a case against abortionists, Nixon's Presidency saw the

---

[41] https://www.lifenews.com/2014/01/23/richard-nixon-abortion-is-necessary-when-you-have-a-black-and-a-white/ (Accessed9/24/22)

enactment of legislation leaving abortion rights as the "law of the land."

"Tapes recently released by the Nixon Presidential Library reveal that President Richard M. Nixon, who had been considered generally opposed to abortion, told aides on January 23, 1973 (the day after the decision was handed down) that abortion was justified in certain cases, such as interracial pregnancies."[42] Nixon's comment, unfortunately, verbalized the morality of many Americans at that time.

"As a matter of fact, one of the dirty secrets of the abortion rights movement is that its earliest momentum was driven by a concern that was deeply racial. Leaders such as Margaret Sanger, the founder of Planned Parenthood, argued quite openly that abortion and other means of birth control were necessary in order to limit the number of undesirable children. As she made clear, the least desirable children were those born to certain ethnically and racially defined families. Sanger, along with so many other "progressive" figures of the day, promoted the agenda of the eugenics movement — more children from the 'fit' and less from the 'unfit.'"[43]

Ruth Bader Ginsburg echoed President Nixon's concerns:

"In an interview published in The New York Times Magazine, Justice Ginsburg made her absolute support of abortion on demand unconditionally clear. She tied her

---
42 Ibid.
43 Ibid.

support for abortion to the larger feminist agenda and lamented the passage of the Hyde Amendment which excludes the use of Medicaid for abortions. The Supreme Court upheld the Hyde amendment in 1980, surprising Ginsburg, who commented: 'Frankly I had thought at the time Roe was decided, there was concern about population growth and particularly growth in populations that we don't want to have too many of. So that Roe was going to be then set up for Medicaid funding for abortion.'"[44]

Nixon was a Republican. Ruth Bader Ginsburg was a Democrat. This was not a "Party-Line" issue at the time. America's morals were (and are) against God's principles. Is it any wonder that God will judge America?

## THE EIGHTH FEATHER

Next up was Gerald Ford who took over when Nixon resigned. Surprisingly, he was a "regular feather" even though he only served three years. But those three years were the balance of Richard Nixon's term. Ford was the only President who had not been elected either President or Vice President.

Nixon's Vice President, Spiro T. Agnew, was forced to resign his office. Nixon then needed the vote of Congress for a new Vice President under the Twenty-Fifth Amendment to the Constitution. He nominated "the only Republican whom

---

[44] https://www.lifesitenews.com/opinion/the-racist-roots-of-roe-v-wade/ , https://www.lifenews.com/2014/01/23/richard-nixon-abortion-is-necessary-when-you-have-a-black-and-a-white/ (Accessed 9/24/22)

the Democratic leadership of Congress would approve, … Jerry Ford."[45]

One of his first acts was conditional amnesty for those who dodged the draft or deserted during the Vietnam War. Then Gerald Ford pardoned Nixon. He tried to cope with the high rate of inflation by slowing down the economy. The result was a severe recession. This lowered the inflation, but unemployment rose to almost nine percent.

During the final days of Vietnam, Ford ordered an airlift of refugees from Da Nang.

With all this, he lost his election bid for the office of President.

## THE NINTH FEATHER

Jimmy Carter was our next President. His biggest accomplishment was a peace deal between Israel and Egypt. He was the most liberal candidate of his time, but he promised "strong moral leadership." After Richard Nixon (and Gerald Ford pardoning him), the American people were receptive to this message.[46] He supported the Civil Rights Movement, which many politicians were against.[47] His

---

45 https://www.britannica.com/biography/Gerald-Ford (Accessed 9/24/22)
46 https://study.com/academy/lesson/jimmy-carter-as-president-election-foreign-policy-accomplishments.html (Accessed 9/24/22)
47 Ibid.

biggest mistake was the Iranian Hostage Crisis. Second was "his inability to successfully deal with the energy crisis."[48]

Under President Carter, the SALT II treaty was signed with Russia. This limited the number of nuclear weapons each country could produce.[49]

President Carter led a boycott of the 1980 Summer Olympics in Moscow to protest Russia's invasion of Afghanistan, and supplied aid to the Afghan rebels. This, unfortunately, set the Afghan people up for dependence on other nations. Not a good situation in God's economy. (Read my next book, Revelation: Where Are We?)

# THE TENTH FEATHER

After President Carter comes Ronald Reagan. He served the full eight years. His goals were to change how the welfare system works for underprivileged Americans, saying he aimed to "send the welfare bums back to work." Now many people may think this is cruel and unusual punishment; but, in God's economy, this is fair. If a man can work, he needs to work.

> *Psalm 104:23 Man goeth forth unto his work and to his labour until the evening.*

---

48 Ibid.
49 https://study.com/academy/lesson/the-salt-treaties-1-2-nuclear-non-proliferation.html (Accessed 9/24/22)

*Isaiah 65:22  They shall not build, and another inhabit; they shall not plant, and another eat: for as the days of a tree are the days of my people, and mine elect shall long enjoy the work of their hands.*

*Galatians 6:4  But let every man prove his own work, and then shall he have rejoicing in himself alone, and not in another.*

*1 Thessalonians 4:11  And that ye study to be quiet, and to do your own business, and to work with your own hands, as we commanded you;*

*2 Thessalonians 3:10  For even when we were with you, this we commanded you, that if any would not work, neither should he eat.*

*2 Thessalonians 3:11  For we hear that there are some which walk among you disorderly, working not at all, but are busybodies.*

*2 Thessalonians 3:12  Now them that are such we command and exhort by our Lord Jesus Christ, that with quietness they work, and eat their own bread.*

*Sirach 7:15  Hate not laborious work, neither husbandry, which the most High hath ordained.*

Reagan ended the Iran Hostage Crises after the Americans had been held for 444 days. This happened the same day he was inaugurated – January 20, 1981.[50] He made sure he started acting as President at once. (No pun intended, since he was a well-known Hollywood actor.)

March 10, 1981, Reagan proposed increasing defense spending and decreasing taxes and domestic spending in his speech to Congress.[51] Inflation at the time was around ten percent.

While many are convinced that this increased income to the Federal Government, the opposite is true. Reagan's tax cut, known as The Economy Recovery Tax Act of 1981, was not able to pay for itself. The Federal Reserve went down by approximately nine percent in the first two years after its enactment. It increased the national debt and budget deficits. Therefore, 1982 – 1987 saw increased tax rates. Future Presidents George H. W. Bush and Bill Clinton had raised the tax rates in 1990 and 1993, respectively.[52]

1982 also saw the "unemployment rate rise above ten percent and the Federal Reserve's war on inflation increased interest rates to nearly twenty percent which caused a severe recession."[53]

---

50 https://millercenter.org/president/ronald-reagan/key-events (Accessed 9/24/22)
51 Ibid.
52 Ibid.
53 https://help.taxreliefcenter.org/reagan-tax-cuts/ (Accessed 9/26/22)

## THE ELEVENTH FEATHER

George H. W. Bush succeeded Reagan as President. He served only four years.

"Bush 41" seemed more interested in Foreign Policy than Domestic Policy. He ordered an invasion of Panama to oust General Manuel Noriega who was known for his involvement in the drug trade and his brutality to the citizens of his country. The invasion was denounced by the UN General Assembly and the Organization of American States.[54]

His Presidency also saw the end of communism in eastern Europe and the Soviet Union and the reunification of Germany.[55]

After Iraq invaded Kuwait in 1990, Bush put an embargo on Iraq and sent troops to Saudi Arabia to counteract Iraq. When Iraq refused to withdraw, the Persian Gulf War started in February 1991 that decimated Iraq's armies and restored Kuwait's independence.[56]

Bush's biggest mistake was reneging on his promise: "Read my lips. No new taxes." In 1990, he raised taxes to try to cope with the budget deficit.[57] Even this did not turn the economy around.

---

54 https://www.britannica.com/biography/George-H-W-Bush/Presidency (Accessed 9/26/22)
55 Ibid.
56 Ibid.
57 Ibid.

# THE TWELFTH FEATHER

Bush lost his reelection bid to Bill Clinton of Arkansas whose campaign kept chanting, "It's the economy, stupid!"

Bill Clinton tried to end discrimination against gay men and lesbians in the military, which was met with criticism from conservatives and some military leaders. What does God have to say about this? And what did God have to say about Clinton's morals? You will see both answers in the following Scriptures:

> *Genesis 1:27-28 So God created man in his own image, in the image of God created he him; male and female created he them. And God blessed them, and God said unto them, Be fruitful, and multiply, and replenish the earth, and subdue it: and have dominion over the fish of the sea, and over the fowl of the air, and over every living thing that moveth upon the earth.*
>
> *Leviticus 18:22 Thou shalt not lie with mankind, as with womankind: it is abomination.*
>
> *Leviticus 20:13a If a man also lie with mankind, as he lieth with a woman, both of them have committed an abomination:*

*Proverbs 5:18-19 Let thy fountain be blessed: and rejoice with the wife of thy youth. Let her be as the loving hind and pleasant roe; let her breasts satisfy thee at all times; and be thou ravished always with her love.*

*1 Corinthians 6:9-10 Know ye not that the unrighteous shall not inherit the kingdom of God? Be not deceived: neither fornicators, nor idolaters, nor adulterers, nor effeminate, nor abusers of themselves with mankind, Nor thieves, nor covetous, nor drunkards, nor revilers, nor extortioners, shall inherit the kingdom of God.*

*1 Corinthians 6:18-19 Flee fornication. Every sin that a man doeth is without the body; but he that committeth fornication sinneth against his own body. What? know ye not that your body is the temple of the Holy Ghost which is in you, which ye have of God, and ye are not your own?*

*Romans 1:26-32 For this cause God gave them up unto vile affections: for even their women did change the natural use into that which is against nature: And likewise also the men, leaving the natural use of the woman, burned in their lust one toward another; men with men working that which is unseemly, and receiving in themselves that recompence of their error which was meet. And even as they did not like to retain God in their knowledge, God gave them over to a reprobate mind, to do those things which are not convenient; Being filled with all unrighteousness, fornication, wickedness, covetousness, maliciousness; full of envy, murder, debate, deceit, malignity; whisperers, Backbiters, haters of God, despiteful, proud, boasters, inventors of evil things, disobedient to parents, Without understanding, covenantbreakers, without natural affection, implacable, unmerciful: Who knowing the judgment of God, that they which commit such things are worthy of death, not only do the same, but have pleasure in them that do them.*

*1 Timothy 1:8-11 But we know that the law is good, if a man use it lawfully; Knowing this, that the law is not made for a righteous man, but for the lawless and disobedient, for the ungodly and for sinners, for unholy and profane, for murderers of fathers and murderers of mothers, for manslayers, For whoremongers, for them that defile themselves with mankind, for menstealers, for liars, for perjured persons, and if there be any other thing that is contrary to sound doctrine; According to the glorious gospel of the blessed God, which was committed to my trust.*

Just for your information, a "whoremonger" is a man who sells himself to other men for sexual purposes.[58]

> *Mark 10: 6-9 But from the beginning of the creation God made them male and female. For this cause shall a man leave his father and mother, and cleave to his wife; And they twain shall be one flesh: so then they are no more twain, but one flesh. What therefore God hath joined together, let not man put asunder.*

## THE THIRTEENTH FEATHER

Next in line was George W. Bush, commonly known as "Bush 43." He served the full two terms.

George W. Bush was used by God to fulfill one of His decrees. God had said that Babylon would never be occupied again.

> *Isaiah 13:19-22 And Babylon, the glory of kingdoms, the beauty of the Chaldees' excellency, shall be as when God overthrew Sodom and Gomorrah. It shall never be inhabited, neither shall it be dwelt in from generation*

---
58 Strong's Hebrew and Greek Dictionaries, Published 1890, public domain.

*to generation: neither shall the Arabian pitch tent there; neither shall the shepherds make their fold there. But wild beasts of the desert shall lie there; and their houses shall be full of doleful creatures; and owls shall dwell there, and satyrs shall dance there. And the wild beasts of the islands shall cry in their desolate houses, and dragons in their pleasant palaces: and her time is near to come, and her days shall not be prolonged.*

*Jeremiah 51:24-26 And I will render unto Babylon and to all the inhabitants of Chaldea all their evil that they have done in Zion in your sight, saith the LORD. Behold, I am against thee, O destroying mountain, saith the LORD, which destroyest all the earth: and I will stretch out mine hand upon thee, and roll thee down from the rocks, and will make thee a burnt mountain. And they shall not take of thee a stone for a corner, nor a stone for foundations; but thou shalt be desolate for ever, saith the LORD.*

*Jeremiah 51:37 And Babylon shall become heaps, a dwellingplace for dragons, an astonishment, and an hissing, without an inhabitant.*

Why are these Scriptures important and how do they relate to President 41?

"[D]uring the Iran-Iraq War, Saddam Hussein became obsessed with the Babylonian ruler Nebuchadnezzar, who is notorious for waging bloody wars to seize large swaths of current-day Iran and Israel. Saddam saw himself as a modern reincarnation of Nebuchadnezzar, and to prove it, he spent millions building a massive reconstruction of Babylon."[59] The former Iraqi leader, who had been president for 24 years, was found by American troops on 13 December 2003 in the town of ad-Dawr, near the city of Tikrit.

"The following day, US president George W Bush announced his capture to the world."[60]

# THE FOURTEENTH FEATHER

This brings us to President Obama and the last feather on this wing. He served two full terms.

Obama bowed to a Muslim king.[61] And yet here in the United States, he professes to be a Christian.

---

59 https://www.atlasobscura.com/articles/babylon-iraq-saddam-hussein (Accessed 9/27/22)
60 https://ca.news.yahoo.com/operation-red-dawn-george-w-bush-capture-saddam-hussein-075542814.html (Accessed 9/27/22)
61 https://www.beliefnet.com/columnists/watchwomanonthewall/2012/02/obama-admits-he-is-a-muslim-in-his-own-words-video.html (Accessed 9/27/22)

He stopped wearing an American Flag pin during his campaign because he was not proud of how the pin has come to represent patriotism in America.[62]

During the Obama administration, Unemployment dropped from ten percent to five percent, which is good. However, "[a] steady hollowing of the middle class, for example, continued during Obama's presidency, and income inequality reached its highest point since 1928." This was bad. "Eight states and the District of Columbia legalized marijuana for recreational purposes."[63]

"[T]he Supreme Court … overturned long-standing bans on same-sex marriage, effectively legalizing such unions nationwide. … [A] majority of Americans said for the first time that they favored same-sex marriage."[64] This was bad. Against God's laws.

> *Genesis 1:26-27 And God said, Let us make man in our image, after our likeness: and let them have dominion over the fish of the sea, and over the fowl of the air, and over the cattle, and over all the earth, and over every creeping thing that creepeth upon the earth. So God created man in his own image, in the image of God created he him; male and female created he them.*

---

62 Ibid.
63 Ibid.
64 https://news.gallup.com/poll/147662/first-time-majority-americans-favor-legal-gay-marriage.aspx (Accessed 9/27/22)

> *Leviticus 18:22 Thou shalt not lie with mankind, as with womankind: it is abomination.*

> *Leviticus 18:24-30 Defile not ye yourselves in any of these things: for in all these the nations are defiled which I cast out before you: And the land is defiled: therefore I do visit the iniquity thereof upon it, and the land itself vomiteth out her inhabitants. Ye shall therefore keep my statutes and my judgments, and shall not commit any of these abominations; neither any of your own nation, nor any stranger that sojourneth among you: (For all these abominations have the men of the land done, which were before you, and the land is defiled;) That the land spue not you out also, when ye defile it, as it spued out the nations that were before you. For whosoever shall commit any of these abominations, even the souls that commit them shall be cut off from among their people. Therefore shall ye keep mine ordinance, that ye commit not any one of these abominable customs, which were committed before you, and that ye defile not yourselves therein: I am the LORD your God.*

So now we have added government-approved homosexuality to government-approved abortion. And we wonder why God is angry!

> *Romans 1:25-27 Who changed the truth of God into a lie, and worshipped and served the creature more than the Creator, who is blessed for ever. Amen. For this cause God gave them*

> *up unto vile affections: for even their women did change the natural use into that which is against nature: And likewise also the men, leaving the natural use of the woman, burned in their lust one toward another; men with men working that which is unseemly, and receiving in themselves that recompence of their error which was meet.*
>
> *Amos 1:13 Thus says the LORD: For three transgressions of the Ammonites, and for four, I will not revoke the punishment; because they have ripped open pregnant women in Gilead in order to enlarge their territory. (NRSV)*

Margaret Sanger started what became Planned Parenthood because she wanted to reduce the population of the Black and brown people. She placed the abortion centers in or close to the black areas so the procedure was easily available to them. This is known as *eugenics*. "Eugenics was a discipline, championed by prominent scientists but now widely debunked, that promoted "good" breeding and aimed to prevent "poor" breeding. The idea was that the human race could be bettered through encouraging people with traits like intelligence, hard work, cleanliness (thought to be genetic) to reproduce."[65] It also, in the hands of a prejudiced person, would prevent those considered "inferior" from reproducing.

---

[65] https://www.npr.org/sections/itsallpolitics/2015/08/14/432080520/fact-check-was-planned-parenthood-started-to-control-the-black-population (Accessed 9/27/22)

Abortion, even sterilization, could be considered to reach this goal.

Both homosexuality and abortion are an abomination to God.

If we go to the interpretation in 2 Esdras 12:18 which concerns the time after the 12 "regular" feathers rule, we find the information in the next chapter.

# CHAPTER 5

## PRESIDENTS AFTER OBAMA

### *2 ESDRAS 12:18*

*2Es 12:18 That after the time of that kingdom there shall arise great strivings, and it shall stand in peril of failing: nevertheless it shall not then fall, but shall be restored again to his beginning.*

### *EXPLANATION*

This concerns the time immediately after Obama's time in office. "There shall arise great strivings." This was fulfilled in the fact that the Democrats were so incensed that an "outsider" should actually win the election that they and the departments they ruled (Department of Justice, the FBI, and the IRS – not to mention the government of New York where he was from) set about trying to oust him. Trump was investigated and impeached – twice. But no criminal activity could be attached to him. Even after he left office, he, at the time of this writing, is being investigated for criminal activity concerning the taking of files. They are even looking into the possibility that he took files to some other property or properties to hide them from the officials.

HOWEVER, "it shall not then fall, but shall be restored again to his beginning." This is talking about the eagle being restored to his beginning.

There is hope. For a while.

### *2 ESDRAS 11:23*

*And there was no more upon the eagle's body, but three heads that rested, and six little wings.*

### *EXPLANATION*

The body had become the "ruling party." That is why the heads rested. Even "rulers" of the opposition party knew that in order to accomplish anything, they had to appease the ruling party. The party that had oppressed the Blacks and the brown populations. The party that started abortion. The party that pushed for the LGBTQ+. (And no, I am not going to put all those other letters in – the "+" is inclusive. I'm just thankful it was someone in that group that decided to add the "Q". If anyone else had done it, it would have been classified as homophobic.).

### *2 ESDRAS 11:24*

*Then saw I also that two little feathers divided themselves from the six, and remained under the head that was upon the right side: for the four continued in their place.*

### *EXPLANATION*

There are several Hebrew words that can be translated into "wing" or into "feather." One is notsah notsah. Another word is kanaph and can also be translated "wing" or "feather." If a translator or scribe were rushed, it would be easy to mistranslate the word by not realizing the context of the word, not just in the sentence, but in the grander context of the passage. That is why we see in verse 23 that it says "six little wings" when what it is talking about is "six little feathers."

A total of 8 "rulers" left to reign, counting the two little feathers that divided themselves from the six and remained "under the head that was on the right side."

## *2 ESDRAS 11:25-26*

*2 Esdras 11:25  And I beheld, and, lo, the feathers that were under the wing thought to set up themselves and to have the rule.*

*2 Esdras 11:26  And I beheld, and, lo, there was one set up, but shortly it appeared no more.*

## *EXPLANATION*

Two of the feathers went under the wing. They hid.

The one who was set up is Trump, who financed his own campaign. Each of these Presidents will be set up by someone – either themselves, or by those who are actually in power.

What happened during Trump's Presidency?

According to University Virginia, Miller Center, the Global Gag Rule, also known as the "Mexico City Policy" was reinstated. This was first introduced in 1984 by Ronald Reagan and it banned aid to international groups performing or counseling about abortion.[66]

---

[66] https://millercenter.org/president/trump/key-events Accessed 9/28/22

The United States withdrew from the Trans-Pacific Partnership. This would help keep manufacturing jobs and raise wages in our nation.[67]

Trump signed an executive order that denied entry for people from Iran, Iraq, Libya, Somalia, Sudan, Syria, and Yemen and suspended the Refugee Admissions policy for 120 days. He later had to lift the ban on Iraqis and permanent US residents in those countries. It also temporarily suspended the Refugee Admission Program.[68]

Trump ordered strikes against an air base in Syria after they launched a chemical weapon attack that killed civilians including children.

The US withdrew from the Paris climate accord.

The kingdom was surely restored again to its beginning. It did not fall. But that will not keep the "heads" from trying.

The time between when Trump was not re-elected and Joe Biden was installed as President was when I was angry. Angry initially because I was watching the returns and saw figures flip in one state. Trump had been ahead. Suddenly

---

[67] https://us.search.yahoo.com/yhs/search?hspart=adk&hsimp=yhs-adk_sbnt&param2=e2924ee4-6c8f-47e2-a1e9-d36a704dc31f&param3=quicksearchtool_3.3.1~US~appfocus1~&param4=d-ccc2-dsf_searchmanager-tst0--lp0-dsf_searchmanager-tst1--bb8~Chrome~what+was+the+TransPacific+Partnership+and+why+was+it+good+for+us+to+withdraw%3f~76AEBBC04C80FDCFB581276FF89F8C50~Win10&param1=20200411&us_privacy=1---&p=what+was+the+TransPacific+Partnership+and+why+was+it+good+for+us+to+withdraw%3f&type=A1-win-~2020-15~ Accessed 9/28/22

[68] https://millercenter.org/president/trump/key-events Accessed 9/28/22

the numbers changed and Biden was given Trump's numbers and vice versa. I asked my husband, "Did you see that?!?"

Then, videos started appearing of people pulling suitcases out from under tables and putting papers through the vote counting machines. More videos of ballot dumps at collection boxes.

But God had used Pharaoh. And other rulers. All to ensure His Word was true. No, I had to be angry with myself because I knew that. But I had hoped for Trump to win.

There is good news. Read my next book, "Bye, Bye, Biden" to discover what the good news is!

# CHAPTER 6

## WHAT HAPPENS TO TRUMP?

We don't know. Plain and simple. BUT God will NOT allow him to be seen as the President of these United States again.

He might consider running for another office. Perhaps the House or the Senate. Surely, if he won, he could be named the Speaker of the House or President Pro Tempore of the Senate.

Don't forget, God uses both good and bad people to accomplish his Word. In Egypt, God used Pharoah as punishment of His people for disobeying His commandments. They had begun to accept various gods the Egyptians worshipped. Witness the Golden Calf they worshipped. Oh, yeah – Aaron said they tossed all their gold into the fire and "out came this calf."[69]

Habakkuk describes how God used Babylon to achieve His purpose.

> *Habakkuk 1:12 Art thou not from everlasting, O LORD my God, mine Holy One? we shall not die. O LORD, thou hast ordained them for judgment; and, O mighty God, thou hast established them for correction.*

This is not to say that God creates sin, just that He controls it.

Not to fear, though. When God gets through using the wicked, He normally destroys them, too.

After using Pharoah, God destroyed him and his army in the Red Sea. And Babylon does not exist anymore, either.

After using Babylon to judge Judah, God destroyed Babylon.

How God chooses to judge is up to Him. But He will judge! His Word is true. Like it or not, it is true.

President Trump, I am begging you not to run. You will never be placed in the office of President again. Should you

---
[69] Exodus 32:24

win re-election, you will not see the light of office. That is NOT a threat from me. It is God's Word. God's Word is true. It will not be mocked. Personally, I wish you would be back in office. The people of this country would be much better off.

You can be "the power behind the throne." You can be the one endorsing other candidates. You can be the one guiding them in what they should do.

Is there anything to prevent you from being the Secretary of State? You can "negotiate" (The Art of the Deal) with heads of countries.

Actually, you can be appointed to any office. God simply said you would not be the ruling person.

So, again, I beg you not to run. Why waste your money? You are a powerful man and you can use that to your advantage – and the advantage of the citizens of these United States.

Thank you for your service as President. You were treated so poorly from the time you were elected – and it continues. We need to get Joe and Kamala out of office and elect a Republican who will pardon you for any crimes you may have done. That is the only thing that will get these swamp members off your back.

It is amazing – you have done nothing wrong, yet they still persist. It goes back to the old adage, "Sling enough mud and something will stick." That's what they are hoping for – something to stick. Meanwhile, they ignore Hunter and Joe and James. The real criminals.

Printed in the USA
CPSIA information can be obtained
at www.ICGtesting.com
LVHW012022191024
794169LV00011B/462